I AM MY SISTER

SHERRY EATON

Dedicated to every woman who has ever felt alone, abandoned, misused, misunderstood, been a misfit, betrayed, or criticized... The Lord has come to set you free in Jesus Name - John 8:32 and whom the Son sets free is FREE indeed, John 8:36

Table of Contents

INTRODUCTION

Fear Nothing Ministries Presents
I AM MY SISTER
Colossians 3: 1-17

Key focus on verses 13-17

In the course of life, we all go through things that makes us feel left alone and misunderstood in singleness, being married and feeling single, being betrayed by loved one, in long term friendships, in church being judged, having to play the role of both parents in a single parent home not having anyone that you can trust or confide in when you're at the end of your rope.

We go as far sometimes to say, "that's none of my business" but if we are Disciples **(learning to follow Jesus)** of Christ, it is our business to be concerned; yet not our business to be overly nosey about the situation. If God leads you to that person to witness or speak life to, please be obedient. Most sisters sit in Lodebar waiting on God because they have not been equipped for storms. God places people in your life for a reason; while they are with you, it is your responsibility to:

A. seek God for that purpose

B. seek God on their behalf. After He has shown you the purpose, you now must act upon it and fulfill it

Also, we have to self-check our own self before we can take on anyone else's cares, concerns and problems. Your life must be an example unto Christ being your head, you are living up to HIS standards and you must have some of the attributes that He has when dealing with your sister (love, joy, peace, longsuffering, gentleness, goodness, faith, meekness, and temperance) Galatians 5:22 & 23

But How Can We Keep One Another?

• We who are strong have an obligation to bear with the failings of the weak, and not to please ourselves. Let each of us please his neighbor for his good, to build him up. For Christ did not please himself, but as it is written, "The reproaches of those who reproached you fell on me" (Rom 15:1-4).

Our care for one another flows out of Christ's care for us. He was strong but became weak for us (Phil 2:5)

He bore with the failings of the weak.

He did not "please himself".

He took our reproach upon himself. He identified with us.

He is not merely our example. He is also our righteousness.

Because we have His righteous record, because we've been completely forgiven and welcomed we are now free to care for others and let them care for us.

We are free to admit our sins and weaknesses to one another. Transparency in relationships flows out of the gospel.

We are free to associate with "sinners".

Compassion for others and their failings flows out of the gospel.

We are free to live selflessly because we've been loved and given everything we need. Selflessness flows out of the gospel because we have everything in Him.

We are now able to be free from comparison, alienation, jealousy, selfish ambition, man-pleasing, fear and self-condemnation.

This particular self-help ministry book will bring openness to the women of God to share, to find solace, to be encouraged and find accountability with past experiences and more importantly the Word of God; you will take on your sister as yourself.(Galatians 6:2)... sharing her pain , her passion , her good days as well as her bad (Romans 12:15).

You will admonish her, guard her, correct her and love her as God leads you (Luke 17:3, 1 Thessalonians 5:14, Ephesians 4:15).

We will NOT work in the flesh; we will listen to the voice of the Holy Spirit to guide our tongues and lead our sister to freedom and keep her in freedom (James 1:19)

As the spirit leads, you will share testimonies that will enhance your sister (Revelation 12:11)

Caring for others begins with your own transparency. Confess your weaknesses and sins weaknesses and sins to one another and ask for prayer and accountability. James 5:16

Last but not least, we will hold confidential group meetings. We ARE NOT to discuss our sister's issues. We are here to help, not sow discord - (Proverbs 6:19)

What does forbearing mean?

in the Greek, anecho "to hold up" (ana, "up," echo, "to have or hold"), signifying "to bear, endure;" it is rendered "forbearing (one another)" in Eph 4:2; Col 3:13.

"You must make allowances for each other's faults and forgive the person who offends you. Remember the Lord forgave you, so you must forgive others." Col. 3:13: (New Living Translation)

There should be times, in which we are to be more concerned about our sisters instead of about ourselves. How can you see one struggling (physically, mentally, economically and especially spiritually) and not feel compassion? Do you remember when it was you wanting to break free from the relationship? from that family member? Do you remember when your man was tearing you down verbally and emotionally? Can you go back to when they placed the eviction notice on your door? Do you remember when your child had you almost on Xanax? Do you recall when you thought you were missing God and needed someone to talk to? Do you remember when you came up pregnant again and still not married? Do you remember when he was bashing you upside the head? Do you remember your time in the courtroom for aggravated assault? Remember when he cheated and got her pregnant?

Don't be so quick to forget what you came through, overcame and walked away from FREE and without residue. You may have some scars, but that is to help you remember, and keep you humble, but you don't have residue: a substance that remains after a process such as combustion or evaporation.

A small amount of something that remains after the main part has gone or been taken or used.

Thank God for our scars (pictures, police reports, hospital diagnosis, negative credit reports or bank accounts) but the residue has been lifted. Yes, I remember but I choose to visit that place ONLY when my sister needs me. I will not make frequent travels to the place that had me almost to the point of suicide. I refuse to think back to where I could have lost my freedom both mentally and physically. The enemy is not allowed to toy with my emotions, and I will not willingly go back to a place that no longer exists.

Chapter 1

~The Woman Caught in Adultery~
(Remember she IS your sister) or is she you?
John 8:1-11

Scribes and Pharisees criticized Jesus and His disciples for NOT keeping the Law and consorting with the sinners.

Can we find ourselves in either one of these groups? If you do, let's examine what you find:

a. Are you being one sided --- this woman was taken in adultery, caught in the VERY act v4, but where was the man?

b. Do you try to twist Scripture or use it to our own advantage v5

c. Do you criticize without examining yourself?

They reminded him of the OLD Law of Moses, (that was done away with) so she should have been stoned.

I was the woman caught in adultery in 1993. I met this guy who I thought was the ideal man- he worked, took care of his daughter and spent quality time with me. Little did I know, he was married! I can hear you now saying, "How did I not know?" He spent mornings with me and most weekends, it's hard to believe he is married, but he was! He made me believe that he wanted to be with me and build our family.

That dream got crushed after numerous encounters of being embarrassed, caught in compromising positions, and such.

When God filled me with His Holy Spirit, I had to go back to that woman after 15 years and ask for forgiveness. There was also another woman that I had to inquire for forgiveness as well. I was so ashamed and so full of guilt. No one ever sat me down and explained to me that I had trespassed, or that I was breaking a covenant between husband and wife. I can hear you saying "duh, they were married" & I got that part!

I didn't understand the power of covenant and how I was now an accomplice to a potential divorce. The statement we were young and dumb does not easily apply. We need sisters who aren't afraid to check, call out, or confront your sister in love.

Thank God that neither woman pulled a gun and blew my brains out as they were entitled to. I had crossed the line with the one they were legally married to. I am thankful for God's hand of protection and His Grace.

Meditation Moment

* Think back to a time when you were accused of something? How did you feel about it? What were your emotions? How did you overcome it (the rumor, the judgment, the anger, the humiliation)?

* Do you see yourself in any of the things mentioned in *Proverbs 6:16-19*? If yes, which ones? and how will you correct them?

*What goals are you making to be a better sister for yourself and for others?

* Relying on God's strength means believing and trusting in His Word, here are few scriptures for memory when you feel your strength has left
   "Since then, we have a great high priest who has passed through the heavens, Jesus, the Son of God, let us hold fast our confession. For we do not have a high priest who is unable to sympathize with our weaknesses, but one who in every respect has been tempted as we are, yet without sin. Let us then with confidence draw near to the throne of grace, that we may receive mercy and find grace to help in time of need."
Hebrews 4:14–16

Psalms 84:5 You bless all who depend on you for their strength

 (***Isaiah 40:31***) NLT...
"Those who trust in the LORD will find new strength. They will soar high on wings like eagles. They will run and not grow weary. They will walk and not faint."

Psalms 71:16 I will go in the strength of the LORD God; I will proclaim your goodness, yours alone. GNB translation

• ***Psalm 46:1-3***, God is our refuge and strength, an ever-present help in trouble.

• ***Proverbs 18:10*** The name of the Lord is a strong tower; the righteous run into it and are safe.
• ***Nehemiah 8:10*** Do not grieve, for the joy of the Lord is your strength.
• Where our strength runs out, God's power begins. Stand in the strength of Jehovah

Chapter 2

~When Your Sister is Accused~
Not only was I accused, I DID IT!!!!

What do you do when someone comes to you about your Sister in Christ? your blood sister? your best friend and pushes accusation off on them? Do you entertain the rumor? *Proverbs 6:16-19*

Proverbs 6:16-19

King James Version (KJV)

16 These six things doth the Lord hate: yea, seven are an abomination unto him:

17 A proud look, a lying tongue, and hands that shed innocent blood,

18 An heart that deviseth wicked imaginations, feet that be swift in running to mischief,

19 A false witness that speaketh lies, and he that soweth discord among brethren.

Do you defend her? Do you say anything? We see here in John 8, verse 7, Jesus flips the script and reminds them that we all have sinned and come short of the Glory of God *Romans 3:23*

We don't know what was written on the ground as Jesus began to write, but whatever it was got their attention! The words He drew caused them to soul search and turn away one by one.

~He who is without sin, cast the first stone~

When your sister is accused, you don't have to bring their sins up, but you can remind them that NO ONE is perfect *Romans 3:10.*

If the Holy Spirit permits, share a personal testimony with them. *Revelations 12:11* King James Version

And they overcame him by the blood of the Lamb, and by the word of their testimony; and they loved not their lives unto death. Let them know that you have been where they are, and God forgave you and restore you.

God has a way of revealing your dirt & skeletons when you try to pull other's skeletons out of the closet. God didn't just let you go through that particular thing for vanity, He predestined you because He knew you could take it. We don't cry out to Jehovah anymore for His strength. John P. Kee has a song that says, He gives me strength, strength to make it, strength to take it, I was strengthened in my spirit when He spoke to me. In the midst of every trial, our strength should be renewed and more powerful than our last test, trial, or storm.

The Greek word *katei* means "power, strength, might."

Who's Power? Whose strength? who's might? God's!!!

I can only be this to someone else through Him.

No matter how strong we think we are, the flesh is always weak. If we lean on our strength, we will fall to temptation and taint God's Glory.

As we learn to rely on God's strength instead of our own, we gain new heights. We learn how to minister more effectively to ourselves and to our sisters.

Psalms 84:5, 7 Blessed are those whose strength is in you, in whose heart are the highways to Zion.

They go from strength to strength; (continuously regain your strength) each one appears before God in Zion.

Always cast your cares, worries, concerns and anxieties onto God for He cares for you *1 Peter 5:7*

Sisters rely on your strength for TODAY and gain new strength on tomorrow. We don't know what tomorrow brings. Let us focus on one day at a time.

Focus on being strong enough for you first, then others. Line up vertically (relationship with God), then spread yourself abroad. We should have a daily regime that consists of prayer, meditation, study of the Word, self-evaluation, and pouring... as you pour out, please let others pour back into you. How depleting to give so much of oneself and go home drained?

2nd Corinthians 12:8-10 And He said to me, "My grace is sufficient for you, for My strength is made perfect in weakness." Therefore, most gladly I will rather boast in my infirmities, that the power of Christ may rest upon me

It's time for sisters to reunite and cry out to God for His strength on behalf of

- broken hearted girls living as grown ups
- battered wives
- molestation and rape victims
- abandoned and rejected women
- sisters who are married but not loved
- sisters who were never mothered

Why do we consort with people when others are going through? Why is it any of our business what they did? We as disciples of Christ who should be there to strengthen, encourage and build up.

If you are not healed emotionally and spiritually, please do not open your mouth to utter one word. The poisonous venom from a broken and bitter woman can hinder your healing and set you back further. Always make sure that you have a circle of ladies that can speak the unadulterated truth to you

IN LOVE and someone who knows the Lord and understand the power of HIS word.

Psalms 107:20

He sent his word, and healed them, and delivered them from their destructions.

God's Word does all things because He is all things. He said in *Exodus 3:14* I AM that I AM! In Hebrew, **Ehye Asher Ehye, I will be who I will be.**

Just as Moses needed to know the name of the Lord to deliver the Israelites from Egypt, you will need to know the appropriate name to assist your sister in her trial. He said He would be whoever we need Him to be... healer, deliverer, redeemer, way maker, provider, protection, etc.

Chapter 3

~Do as Jesus Did~

When we sin, we should always run to the loving and forgiving arms of Jesus, but instead we run to our family, friends and leadership...

What can they do? be nosey? pray? look at you crazy? say I told you so? Instead, run to the One who can not only forgive you, heal you and restore you but God can replenish you.

Interrupt the pattern of what you would normally do!!!

Replenish - fill something up (again) restore to a former level or condition.

Regardless of what we have endured, God is always there with arms wide open to welcome us back to the sheepfold. Matthew 18:12-17

Just as Jesus loved us enough to leave the 99 and go look for the 1, we should be on the same mission. We as women, when we are going through, do one of two things.

We act out or we withdraw.

This scripture speaks of the withdrawing. There is one sheep who has left the sheepfold and went on its way. This reminds me of the time I found out my husband had been cheating with someone in my face. He introduced me to her and let her befriend me while they were having sex behind my back. The whole town knew and only a few reached out to me with concerns.

When reality hit, the first thing I thought was maybe I deserved it; after all, I had slept with other women's husbands in the past. Then, I felt shameful and like everyone was looking at me as "poor Sherry". I wasn't rooted and grounded in the Word and let those feelings of condemnation come over me. I crept into depression and fell into a slump that I really didn't think I would recover from.

I contemplated things in my mind that I should not have. It took me many years to rid myself of the anger, resentment and bitterness that I felt towards him. She did come back and apologize for all the indiscretions.

It was a sister of mine, 939 miles away that made calls to ensure that I was in a good space. Not only did she call but she prayed, and she ministered from a place of her own story.

She saw me.

She remembered the pain.

She revisited the past.

She met me in my need and spoke HOPE & LIFE back into my life.

She made sure my daily routine wasn't interrupted and for the rest of my life, I will be thankful to Tina Henderson for her devoted love and attention to me in that low place. If it wasn't the GOD in her and her commitment to me, I don't know if I would have overcome and had this testimony.

He sent her to come after the ONE. The ONE was me.

I then had the opportunity later to pay it forward. It was the best feeling to help someone else. God empowered me to come through it, then minister to others at their point of need. Have you ever seen a sister in need and saw yourself? What did you do? Did you reach out? Did you pray? Did you withdraw and say, "Oh she will figure it out, I did!"

It is your duty to administer help IF God has delivered you from someone or something. Woe unto you if you left your sister stranded and broken. Even if you feel like you don't have the essential tools to fully help her, a listening ear will at least be the beginning.

#Nosisterleftbehind

There are a lot of empowered women out there who can assist us when we are hurting. Yes, us! I still hurt, I still get low, I still get in a place of looking in the past and I still have regrets with some things I did and allowed in life. I have a few sisters that I can call, and they will pray with me, encourage me, and direct me back to the place of abundance.

NO Sister Left Behind

To be uncovered and unloved is the worst feeling in the world. The enemy is sitting on your chest, and you can't breathe, you need some help and have no one to call.

Yes, we know that Jesus is the realest name to call when life has beat us down, but can I be 100? A lot of us want someone in the natural to pour our hearts out to! We want someone that we can talk to immediately, and they will answer back.

We want someone that will console us in our times of need. Do you have a true sister that you can trust with your innermost feelings? You know that stuff you've kept to yourself because you are ashamed of it and surely don't want to share with anyone else.

Who can you be YOU around?

It's hard to express yourself and still be saved. People are quick to judge you when you say I love the Lord and they see you being your human self. They don't understand that the soul is talking, and through this old nasty flesh, it speaks. We are humans, and we will be that until the Father sends for His investment in the Earth, but at the same time, the soul is who we are seeking to be daily. Our desire should be to please the Father and give Him a sincere yes.

It seems hard to remain faithful during the time of spiritual warfare or trials, but the Lord provides pure spiritual milk and meat to sustain us during this time.

Are you ready to war for your sister? Then put on the whole armor of God

Ephesians 6:11-18 King James Version (KJV)

11 Put on the whole armour of God, that ye may be able to stand against the wiles of the devil.

12 For we wrestle not against flesh and blood, but against principalities, against powers, against the rulers of the darkness of this world, against spiritual wickedness in high places.

13 Wherefore take unto you the whole armour of God, that ye may be able to withstand in the evil day, and having done all, to stand.

14 Stand therefore, having your loins girt about with truth, and having on the breastplate of righteousness.

15 And your feet shod with the preparation of the gospel of peace.

16 Above all, taking the shield of faith, wherewith ye shall be able to quench all the fiery darts of the wicked.

17 And take the helmet of salvation, and the sword of the Spirit, which is the word of God:

18 Praying always with all prayer and supplication in the Spirit and watching thereunto with all perseverance and supplication for all saints.

The armour that is available for believers to put on is God's own armour (*Isaiah 59:16–19*), for He is the Divine Warrior. DO NOT let the enemy cause you and your sister to miss the deliverance that God sent His only Begotten Son to die for.

Romans 8:13 King James Bible

For if ye live after the flesh, ye shall die: but if ye through the Spirit do mortify the deeds of the body, ye shall live.

Who is it that I can live around when I mortify the deeds of the body?

Who can I show my scars, show my craziness to show my weaknesses, and still be the child of God? I need HER when I'm vulnerable.

Being sisters create a bond to enhance you in times of need. ***Romans 15:1*** says, "let the strong bear the infirmities of the weak."

You don't get to overcome your trials and then proceed in life without going back to help others. That is the reason why God made you an overcomer. There is grace over your trial to make sure you understood the fullness of setting the captive free and the strength to endure. We as women get tired and want to give up, but we can't. The fact that we are nourishers is the strength we need to endure past circumstances and situations.

Endurance isn't meant for the weak or the faint at heart but to the one with a made-up mind. I will not let anything the enemy throws my way (through God's permission) to move me off course.

Ecclesiastes 9:11 I returned and saw under the sun, that the race is not to the swift, nor the battle to the strong, neither yet bread to the wise, nor yet riches to men of understanding, nor yet favour to men of skill; but time and chance happeneth to them all.

The Lord has blessed us with intellect, wisdom, and reasoning. He has developed a healing mechanism that comes in effect in case the body is attacked by sickness or other factors that try to weaken the body. Many may have holy hands at work, with closed spiritual ears that are reluctant to hear and obey the Lord. Hear the Lord concerning your sister's needs and desires.

She is hungry and thirsty as well for more in the Spirit, more sisterly love and more of a relationship. Don't turn a deaf ear to her. Learn to war in the Spirit on her behalf until she gets what she has asked of the Lord.

Hezekiah Walker has a song that says, "I need you; you need me. We're all a part of God's Body. Stand with me. Agree with me. We're all a part of God's body. It is HIS will that every need be supplied. You are important to me; I need you to survive".

Next time you look in your sister's face, hear her saying I need you to survive. I need your testimony, your strength, your endurance to make it.... And fight for her as if it's your life!

Meditation Moment

Recall a moment that had you at your lowest, and you overcame it.

What do you do with that moment? Do you pack it away and move on with life, or do you share with others when the Holy Spirit prompts you to?

Have you examined that moment and let the Lord minister to you?

Have you prayed from that place of Hurt, Anger, Disappointment?

Am I willing to face reality?

Did forgiveness come, OR are you still holding onto it?

Are you in a healed place to minister and comfort your sister?

Galatians 6:1
Darby Bible Translation
Brethren, if even a man be taken in some fault, ye who are spiritual restore such a one in a spirit of

meekness, considering thyself lest thou also be tempted.

John 14:18 I will not leave you comfortless, I will come to you

Get rid of all bitterness, rage, and anger, brawling and slander, along with every form of malice. Be kind and compassionate to one another, forgiving each other, just as in Christ God forgave you."
Ephesians 4:31-32

Being Spiritually stranded is like being on the side of the road without a spare tire... you have to sit and wait for help to come

Chapter 4

~Sisterhood is a Not A Destination but A Journey~

Lead Her (Ship) - vessel used for transporting people or goods.

Leadership

Taking on the role of your sister can be a tough and difficult task; you must hear the Lord speak to you to move in this area. Stepping into her shoes, her role, her lifestyle WILL NOT be easy, but if God ordained you for such a time as this; the task will be worth it.

Leading her ship means getting in the ship with her... children issues, demonic attacks, financial struggles, Spiritual struggles, and whatever else she may be facing.... ARE YOU WILLING TO GET IN THE BOAT? ARE YOU EQUIPPED FOR WARFARE? WILL YOU STAY WITH HER UNTIL THE END?

A ship is a large thing to steer.

When we first moved to Wilmington, NC we went to tour the USS Battleship because my son wanted to join the Navy. It took us almost 45 minutes to complete the tour. There were 4 levels on this ship with many rooms. As with your sister, she will have many levels (good days, bad days, quiet days, sad days she doesn't want to be bothered days) and a lot of rooms or struggles, issues, worries, concerns, anxieties, etc.

In each room, you may meet a different person, in the kitchen she may be the quiet reserved sister who doesn't speak because her husband criticizes everything she cooks.

In the bedroom, she may be outlandish and perverse because that is where her uncle first introduced her to sex,; in the bathroom, she may be loud because that was the only place she could go to escape and cry out in pain.

This assignment is not a one and done thing, this is a LIFETIME commitment, just as addicts have relapse and need a sponsor, your sister will suffer from those until she is strong enough to endure it.

Anniversary dates, certain scents, a specific song, a memory on their Facebook timeline... when it's his weekend with the kids and she has to see him, holidays that are too hard to face, etc. Are you up for the task of becoming your sister?

You can't roll your eyes every time the phone rings, remember when it was you! I utterly understand what I laid on other's plates. I thank God they were patient enough and equipped enough to steer me into a right place.

In this vessel is where you will have to check yourself and your relationship with God. I would not recommend getting into this sisterSHIP or being an accountability partner if you are not completely healed from your past hurts.

Hurting People Hurt People, but remember Healed People Heal People, also.

Your sister will rely on you for a lot of moral and spiritual support, please be honest enough to say, "I am not ready to support you" if that is the case. You can refer her to someone else. We don't want to send anyone into relapse if they aren't strong enough.

I have a client, let's call her Sarah. She is dealing with seeing White Lexus cars. Her ex, Chris was having an affair with someone who was her but a different race. Mary (not real name) and Sarah worked together and had a great relationship over the span of 8 years. They had endured a lot of life together. True enough, they were not best friends, but they hung out once a month for a Girls Day Out.

Sarah started dating Chris about 3 years ago and noticed that his routine was changing. She didn't pay it any attention until Mary started traveling to the place that she and Chris had gone as a couple. She began to look more closely into his phone calls, texts, bank statements, to her surprise, Chris and Mary were in a secret affair. Chris purchased Mary the same car as he did Sarah, a white Lexus GS 350.

Sarah's whole life changed in the blink of an eye when she demolished both vehicles and set them on fire at a private resort. Truth is, we never want to believe the one we love would ever cause us harm in any area.

We know ladies, that some people can take us to a point of no return. A moment cost Sarah her job, her sanity and her freedom. Yes, she went to prison for felony damage of property and assault for 4 years. She stated if she had someone to call and talk to at that moment, it could have saved her life.

permission granted to use story

So, my question to her was, who was guiding your ship when you argued with Chris?

Who was monitoring what cargo was being loaded onto your ship?

How often did you do an inventory of the things on your ship? RelationSHIP, FriendSHIP, Business PartnerSHIP?

What kind of water did the ship rest in? Tap, Filtered, Distilled

Distilled water doesn't contain any impurities (waste, lies, deceit)

Filtered water has the impurities removed by lowering the contamination process of chemicals.

Your SHIP can be built with the finest of things and people, but if it sits in contaminated waters, it will begin to rust, deteriorate and lose its value.

Leadership (Pastor, Ministers, Bishops) are there to lead you, but you **MUST** have a relationship with Christ for yourself. I petition every leader that is reading this book to get some type of counseling or Life Coaching under your belt to deal with the severity of your congregation being broken, bringing profound teaching to your services for unity in sisterhood, dealing with the whole man (mind, body, soul, will and emotions) and teaching Self Care to every member that you have.

#SUPPORT SYSTEM

We as women are the worst at supporting one another in ANYTHING, but especially in church... in Kingdom Building & Marketplace. We get the crab syndrome quick, don't wanna see each other prosper, don't wanna see one another grow. True enough, we were created equal, but that doesn't mean I have to stay where you are. The Bible encourages us to grow in the Grace and Knowledge of our Lord and Savior Jesus Christ. To Him be the glory, both now and forever Amen, *2 Peter 3:18*

On this journey, a lot of people I had to detach from. It hurt, but I knew that if I continued to be in that circle, I would resort back to my old ways. I wasn't strong enough to be in that atmosphere and still do the work of the Lord.

Jesus told this woman, "Neither do I condemn you; go, and sin no more v 11

After that, He didn't remind her of the things she had done, He didn't say " this is the 5th time that I have forgave you"

No! He just simply told her that I don't condemn you..... when our sisters confide in us, we are **NOT** to condemn, we are to encourage them.

That word encourage breaks down to en- "within, in," occurring in loanwords from Greek: energy; enthusiasm.

Courage - the ability to do something that frightens one OR strength in the face of pain or grief.

So, look within yourself and find the courage to face your fears, disappointments, your hurts and then move forward.

Meditation Moment

Who is in your sisterhood?
What ship(s) are you boarding with them?
What type of water(s) are they producing for your
ship(s)?

1 Thessalonians 5:12
And we urge you, brethren, to recognize those who
labor among you, and are over you in the Lord and
admonish you

Ezekiel 36:25-27
25 I will sprinkle clean water on you, and you will
be clean; I will cleanse you from all your impurities
and from all your idols. 26 I will give you a new
heart and put a new spirit in you; I will remove
from you your heart of stone and give you a heart
of flesh. 27 And I will put my Spirit in you and
move you to follow my decrees and be careful to
keep my laws

Be mindful of the CREW members on your boat.
Coming
Receiving
Elevating
Working

Chapter 5

~The Sister as a Woman~

At the age of around thirteen, our bodies and minds begin to change. We as women begin to develop, and we have new emotions and feelings. We are unsure of what is going on, with the wrong guidance the newness in our lives can be tainted in many areas.

I personally feel it is the mother's responsibility to guide that daughter into her new place with love, understanding and care. The lessons we impart into our daughters in these tender years are vital. No other woman outside the family should be investing in this phase. If you are a mother and feel you cannot do the guiding, please seek assistance so your daughter will not go in the wrong way.

My adolescent years weren't the best, my mother imparted some structure into me but there were a lot of areas she left uncovered. In doing so, I was lost for many years and looked for love in all the wrong places.

Oh, don't get me wrong, she taught me how to cook, sew, take care of home, make canned preserves, dress and coordinate, but I didn't know my self-worth and had low self-esteem. It took me many years to come into the knowledge of who I was. I don't totally blame her, I really don't; but I can say it took a lot of my respect from her.

It is essential that our daughters are poured into mentally and spiritually first. The words spoken into a child molds them for greatness or destruction. Why spiritually you ask? The Word of God says before the foundation of the world, God placed dreams, visions and ideas into our spirit man so that we may carry out His Glory in this Earth.

Ephesians 1:4-6

If we as parents are lined up with God's plan, then we can align our children in the right way to go. I understand we get older; we start smelling ourselves and think we know everything, but the truth be told, the prayers of parents lead the children back to God.

Proverbs 22:6 Train up a child in the way he should go, and when he is old, he will not depart from it.

If we don't set the standard for our little girls they will be miserable, misguided old women. What are we investing into them at 4? 12? 18? 21? 25?

After a bad breakup? failed marriages? God's way of living?

Is the environment conducive for impartation?

We must learn the seasons in which our children need to be shifted. Our words must be honey off our lips to their ears! I am guilty that I inherited a lot of my mother's words and passed them onto my daughter. The Lord had to show me as she entered her teenage years that I was repeating the cycle. I quickly repented and began a new regime with her. Was it easy? No, not at first, but I made a vow that I would not sow those hurtful words into her life as they had been planted and rooted into my life.

I assured my daughter she was beautiful and smart.

#Confession, my daughter has a learning disability, but I never used that against her. I would explain to her, she would have to do things differently from the other kids, but we can get it done. Her Jr High and High School years were NOT easy. Thank God, she had people praying to push her into the next phase of life. She graduated in June 2019 from High school. It was a rough road, but she did it. She said "Mama, this is one of my biggest accomplishments" I had to remind her that life would throw her many more stones, but she needed to keep the drive and determination she had, and everything will be fine.

With our sons, we have to take on a role that was never intended for us to carry in order for them to be great. I will not bash men in this book, but I will say that it is a sad shame that Black women have to raise Black boys into Black men alone. Our sons are the seed carriers and our daughters are the nurturers of that seed. They need the love, guidance and admonition of both parents. We do the absolute best we can with the knowledge and wisdom that God gives us, but the children need both parents.

Ephesians 6:4 King James Version (KJV)

4 And ye fathers, provoke not your children to wrath: but bring them up in the nurture and admonition of the Lord.

I thank God for the other women who have poured into me, in different seasons. I will never take away from the next woman who can advance my daughter if I can't. My prayer has been for my daughter that God sends her Holy Spirit friends and mentors. I AM woman enough to say my daughter and I don't see eye to eye on a lot of things, but I know she needs that coaching from someone else whom she will listen to. I can remove myself and let God do the work in that area, even if it doesn't come from me. A lot of women received teaching from other powerful women who were not even related to them. Be wise enough to let your children get their healing and deliverance elsewhere if you can't give it to them. I would be a fool to let my children stay bound knowing I can't deliver them.

There are a lot of women right now who are hurting and desiring change and deliverance. They have been waiting on Mama, Grandma, Auntie, cousins to be free with the truth, but will have to get that freedom, deliverance and healing outside the family. We are not being honest about what's in the bloodline and people are going through emotional and spiritual bondage because Grandma won't be real about what happened. The phrase "what goes on in the house stays in this house" is not a good concept to teach your kids. You are telling them to keep secrets that will mess them up for the next 10,20, or 30 plus years. It's time for my sisters to be free, in Jesus Name. I beg you to break the generational curses in your bloodline, for your sake and your future generations sake.

The Word says in *Luke 12:53* King James Version (KJV)

The father shall be divided against the son, and the son against the father; the mother against the daughter, and the daughter against the mother; the mother in law against her daughter in law, and the daughter in law against her mother in law. It is the enemy's ploy to destroy family, unity (union), our job is to fight for the very thing God has blessed us with.

If we haven't seen love demonstrated then we do not know what love looks like, so when it's time for us to "fall in love" we are lost. We are left wide open for contaminated seeds to be planted. Who or what do you pattern love after? As you were growing up did you see love demonstrated in the home? amongst the family? OR did you see commotion, disrespect and unfaithfulness? This is what you or your children will look for when it's time to pursue a relationship. Trust me, you don't want your children with this misconception over your heads. Find an older couple to mentor you and pour into you and your significant other if you do not know what love, relationships, and marriage looks like.

Meditation Moment

Who are you as a woman?
Who are you as a sister?
Be honest and transparent, how are you
Physically?
Mentally?
Emotionally?
Spiritually?
Financially?

How are your relationships with friends and family?

Write their names and rate them; if they need work, please do the work.
Have you forgiven yourself?

My favorite song to listen to at least 3 times a year is "I'm Sorry" by Kelly Price. Please head over to YouTube and listen. Let is minister to you and then record your thoughts below..

Chapter 6

~As A Mother...~

It's a sad thing to see but there are a lot of single mothers out here doing it alone. I know you didn't see your life as a single mother years ago. I am not speaking to the ones who get the mental, physical and the substantial financial support, but I am speaking to the ones who are truly doing it alone.

In the **United States** today, there are nearly 13.6 million **single parents** raising over 21 million children. **Single** fathers are far less common than **single mothers**, constituting 16% of **single-parent** families.

We must examine ourselves ladies and get to the root of how this happened. Many will say it's because Daddy was absent from the home. Others may say, there was no parental guidance to steer the young lady into adulthood. Then there is a slim chance that we thought we were grown and knew how to walk into life without being steered. Whatever the case may be, it is a fact that we have a lot of single mothers out here raising young men and women by themselves. ... or without support from the fathers.

The things we engage in as teens and young adults will definitely find its way to us in our latter years. I will always be the first to expose me; therefore, I lived a very outlandish lifestyle resulting in 3 kids by 3 different men. I love my children, let it be known! They changed my life in different seasons, and I couldn't be more thankful. My life graduated into another level with each of their births.

As a young girl, I often said I wanted 3 kids- 2 boys and a girl just as my Mama had. I did not wait until a man pursued me and went to my parents and asked for my hand in marriage. I was a broken little girl who was looking for love.

He healed that brokenness, rejection, and fear in my life so I may fully enjoy life abundantly. John 10:10b. Over the course of the years, I was not fit to love anyone. I jumped from endless relationship to relationship. I looked for the love that I so desperately wanted in men and the security of marriage. I poured myself into money, education, trips and even broken people that were worse off than me. I became an enabler to many, I felt like because I was damaged, I couldn't give the advice, love or hope to anyone else. I slept with other women husbands, I crept in circles of conniving women, I was an alcoholic by the age of 18, I was a kleptomaniac who would steal your shirt off your back, I dabbled in credit card fraud, I was introduced to pornography at an early age and addicted to watching it until my late 30's.... while ministering to the Body of Believers.

I am My Sister.

Wilson, NC March 23, 1997, I was at a Youth Revival at Glory Baptist Church when the Holy Spirit arrested me. He filled me that night and my life was never the same. I fell in love truly that night. It was a feeling that no man could ever give me. I spoke in an unknown tongue to the Lover of My Soul. My life changed that night, but I went back to a place 2 years later that was not good for me. It was here that I backslid. The Scripture says Jeremiah 3:14 "Return, O backsliding children," says the Lord; "for I am married to you. Thank God that His Word is true. He never left me even though I left him. I allowed myself to return to the person I was in the same environment that I was broken in.

When God delivers you from a person, place or thing, do everything in your power to stay delivered. God was calling me higher and higher, but my flesh was being drawn back to the lustful things that had me consumed before. I fought hard but not hard enough. I fasted, I prayed, I cried out and I asked for advice but all I had to do was MAKE A CHOICE and stand IN it.

We make our life so hard, when God is saying seek me and let me lead you. This is the way to go. Yes, there will be times when we will have to seek wise counsel, BUT there will also be times when all you have to do is MAKE A CHOICE. See the Holy Spirit sustains you - Psalms 54:4 Surely God is my help; the Lord is the one who sustains me. He will keep (sustain) you if you abide in Him. I hear people say the Holy Spirit will keep you if you wanna be kept. I have to disagree, if you are walking in the way of God, you DO want to be kept, so you can carry out the assignment for His Glory.

Once again, the struggle comes when the CHOICE isn't made. Matthew 15:8 This people honoureth me with their lips: but their heart is far from me. This was me for so many years, lip service unto God, when in actuality, he wants what's in the heart (soul).

In April 2010, I made the choice in my bathroom one Saturday night. After being celibate 10 months, I let the flesh lead me back to an old flame. He wasn't for me then, surely wasn't for me now. I was lonely again; I was desperate again. I sat in my bathroom on the toilet and said "Lord, I am so tired of giving myself to men that aren't concerned about my destiny, my calling or my children. I will wait on you to send me the unexpected. I trust you to send me who you Will for my life." I went on to say "You have called me to deliver women, how can I do so when I am not fully delivered? Father, use me, I surrender to the Will you have for me."

I then laid on the floor and cried out to God to keep me. That night was my game changing moment.

I had a soul exchange with my Creator and My Father.. My life has not been the same since.

It is sad to say I didn't have a sister that I could rely on then to agree with me for celibacy. I was called crazy, people asked "why would you do that to yourself?"

Some made jokes about it and said because of my past, I wouldn't be celibate long.

In making that decision, I did not know then what God had in place. I just knew I was tired of giving myself to men and still feeling empty and alone after the sex. I made the decision.

God didn't threaten me. The prophet didn't come with a Rhema word. I didn't have a dream. I just made a choice.

When you are physically, mentally and spiritually tired, you will decide so that peace and wisdom can find its way into your spirit.

The last 8 years haven't been easy, but I have kept my vow to God in celibacy. The sacrifices to fully surrender have been great. I lost a lot of friends, family turned their backs on me, I had to walk away from ministries, I even had to leave my home state of Texas to pursue this call into destiny. I do not regret anything in life because it has strengthened me, but it has prepared me and the people I encounter to receive so much from God.

Medication Moment

I changed this to MEDICATION because there are some moments in being a parent that we must take our medicine to deal with each child.

Vitamins are essential to the body, and I would like for you as a Mother to apply these to your daily intake of supplements.

Vitamin C - Care
Always let them know you care. Show up for them by supporting them.

Vitamin D - Devotion & Determination
As children see you devoted and determined, this will teach them the same. Set morals and standards for them, the world is lacking it.

Vitamin L - Love & Listen
if you have daughters, I understand these 2 may not mix in your household. You can love them and not like their ways, always make sure they know you love them.

Listen attentively and respond from a place of understanding. Remember, it used to be you or could have been you at that age. Use your experience to interrupt the patterns.

Vitamin T- Talk
Always make time to talk to your children. Instill in them the essential things.
Prayer
Money Management
Conduct
Life Skills
Safety

Vitamin O – Openness

Your past may not be pretty, but I promise you it will be helpful. Keeping secrets and harboring truths from your children will not advance their future. Remember, they are a part of you, and what you don't confront, heal from and kill will find its way into your children or grandchildren's lives. Never let your children hear from the street about your past. You make sure they get the original track and not the remix.

What does your life as a Mother say to your children?

Chapter 7

~The Sister as A Wife~

Oh, we love the fact that our last name is changing, and we are marrying our best friend. It's a lot more to be his wife and having a lavish ceremony. Sisters, if you are not ready to compromise, please do not marry. It breaks my heart that the Body of Christ has not set single women aside and began to prepare them for a life changing moment into covenant.

The marriage between man and woman, should be symbolic of that between Christ and the Church.

Have you truly acknowledged the battles that will come with this marriage?

Do you understand that your body is no longer your own?

Did you consider that he is the first priority, under God to you now?

Are you truly willing to submit to him? After all, he is the head of your household now.

Is his relationship with God rooted and grounded?

Here's another secret about me :) I have been married twice. My first time around I was looking for a Rescue Ranger. He was 9 years older than me and in the military. We were both broken and not ready for marriage. Two broken people does not make the marriage whole, but 2 whole and completed people will. Six years later, we were parting ways and two little boys would have to start their lives without a Daddy.

My second marriage I heard the Lord speak but wanted to be married so bad, I didn't wait to hear God finish the conversation. Times and seasons are crucial when a prophetic word comes. I do believe the humiliation I faced was due to being out of order and moving ahead of God in that marriage.

I often beat myself up about the choices I have made in men, then I am reminded of you my sisters. I went through all of this to tell you, "YOU CAN MAKE IT AND YOU CAN BE BETTER!"

God knew every detail of my life before I took one breath in the world and it is all for His Glory and my good (Romans 8:28) oh trust me it doesn't feel good but it's WORKING for my good. The old saints used to say we will understand it better, by and by, when the morning comes. You know that morning is just a new revelation? It's not the physical sunrise of a new day, and guess what, you decide when your morning comes. We must stop saying "I am waiting on God", no dear heart He is waiting on you.

I am a Woman of Strength because I have the Strength of a Woman!!! That's a profound statement. A woman is powerful all in herself.

When God created women, he was working late on the 6th day.......

An angel came by and asked." Why spend so much time on her?"

The Lord answered. "Have you seen all the specifications I have to meet to shape her?"

She must function on all kinds of situations,

She must be able to embrace several kids at the same time,

Have a hug that can heal anything from a bruised knee to a broken heart,

She must do all this with only two hands, "She cures herself when sick and can work 18 hours a day"

THE ANGEL was impressed "Just two hands.....impossible!

And this is the standard model?"

The Angel came closer and touched the woman

"But you have made her so soft, Lord".

"She is soft", said the Lord,

"But I have made her strong. You can't imagine what she can endure and overcome."

"Can she think?" The Angel asked...

The Lord answered. "Not only can she think she can reason and negotiate."

The Angel touched her cheeks....

"Lord, it seems this creation is leaking! You have put too many burdens on her"

"She is not leaking...it is a tear" The Lord corrected the Angel...

"What's it for?" Asked the Angel......

The Lord said. "Tears are her way of expressing her grief, her doubts, her love, her loneliness, her suffering and her pride." ...

This made a big impression on the Angel,

"Lord, you are a genius. You thought of everything.

A woman is indeed marvelous"

Lord said. "Indeed, she is.

She has strength that amazes a man.

She can handle trouble and carry heavy burdens.

She holds happiness, love and opinions.

She smiles when she feels like screaming.

She sings when she feels like crying, cries when happy and laughs when afraid.

She fights for what she believes in.

Her love is unconditional.

Her heart is broken when a next-of-kin or a friend dies but she finds strength to get on with life"

The Angel asked: "So she is a perfect being?"

The lord replied: "No. She has just one drawback

She often forgets what she is worth."

Many of us got into these situations because we don't know who we are as women, we don't know who we are in God.

There is a famous song that has a line stating, "I Am Woman, hear me roar", this is what our unity should sound like! A pride of lionesses in the wilderness roaring and shaking the very atmosphere, region and climate in which we represent. The very thought of women coming together with one agenda, one voice should make every demon in hell tremble.

Ephesians 4:16 NLT

"He makes the whole body fit together perfectly. As each part does its own special work, it helps the other parts grow, so that the whole body is healthy and growing and full of love."

The Scripture says GOD makes the whole body fit together perfectly, not you!

The King James Version says, from whom the whole body fitly joined together and compacted by that which every joint supplieth, according to the effectual working in the measure of every part, maketh increase of the body unto the edifying of itself in love.

Every joint supplieth (the "eth" suffix means continuously) one bone meets up or fuse (join or blend) with another is the joint

Let's go to verse 11, He says I am the Light of the World; he who follows Me shall not walk in darkness but shall have the Light of Life. Now He shows her who He is; as with us, when we listen to others and hear their compassion, anger, lust, depression, bitterness, then we must turn them back to the Light, which is Jesus. He can take any emotion and make it work for Good.

Sister Be the Light! Save the world from darkness.

Becoming a wife requires more than just lying on your back and giving head to your husband. A wife of substance requires you to listen, be submissive, forsake yourselves sometimes, give up all rights as a single woman, and become a prayer warrior.

You must understand I am not just talking to just any wife, but a GODLY wife who knows her role in the marriage. If you have an issue with submission and servitude, you are dismissed from wanting a marriage.

These two roles will always be on the forefront, whether you like it or not.

Serving your husband as lord, not LORD!

1 Peter 3:6

Honor, love, and Serve him -as Sarah obeyed Abraham, calling him lord, whose daughters you are if you do good and are not afraid with any terror.

Strong's Greek 2962: lord, master, sir.

She merely reverenced him with humility and authority to direct the affairs of his household, and that it was her duty to be in subjection to him as the head of the family. In what respects this is a duty, may be seen by consulting the notes at *Ephesians 5:22*

I do not understand why most women loath the word submission but say they want a husband. No, you are not ready! Marriage is about compromise, sacrifices, and servanthood. True, we are not our mothers and grandmothers, but we can definitely learn a few things from them on how to be a wife.

Honor your husband, as you were the one that chose him. Yes, I will agree that women may do the most work to sustain the marriage, but there is an easy way to do so.

1 Corinthians 7:14

For the unbelieving husband IS sanctified by the wife, and the unbelieving wife is sanctified by the husband; otherwise, your children would be unclean, but now they are holy.

My question is, how is your sanctification?

Sanctification - set apart TO GOD, He is your first love and husband (*Isaiah 54:5*)

Your marriage to God will have an impact on your marriage in the flesh. The time that you spend in the presence, getting instructions on how to be a wife to YOUR husband will either impact or destroy your marriage.

Let me put this footnote here. You are NOT to be in the presence of God more than you are in the presence of your husband; in that case, you should have stayed single.

The Word tells us through the Apostle Paul in

1 Corinthians 7:33-35, if you remain alone, you are to be concerned with the things of the Lord, a married person must be involved with the characteristics of the family.

The order is:

God

Husband

Wife

Children

Family

Ministry

Church

My Sister as The Rib

Why did God choose the rib? The rib is design for three functions, to protect the heart, to protect the lung, and to allow the spine to remain straight.

The Lord is in control of the breathing, which allows the individual to inhale and exhale without any complications. So that there's no out of control breathing, it doesn't escape the bodily organs themselves. In order for a man to function correctly, he needs the proper circulation of breath and exhaling. The right rib won't suffocate a man (her husband) she will give him room and allow him to operate and move freely;

while in the same token bringing your support to his ability to function and circulate properly in operation.

The heart is designed to protect areas of blood flow and continue to give existence to. A man that has its core protected by the rib gives him the ability to trust without any broken heartedness. A right rib protects the heart of a husband; it allows him to be able to trust what comes out without it being damaged or going into cardiac arrest because the rib protects the heart.

The spine. This part is a support system that keeps the nervous system aligned properly without the real connection to the spine, with no balance that could be no proper structure and proper ability to walk and flow freely. The rib allowed the man to walk upright and does not cause him to be in a deformed state of stance. This rib creates an inability to support the human body properly without any sag or bend.

~Alvino Bell~

You (wife) are his Ezer-suitable helper

Genesis 2:18

And the LORD God said, it is not good that the man should be alone; I will make him a help meet H5828 (Hebrew) for him.

And the LORD God said, It is not good that the man should be alone; I will make him a help meet H5828 (Hebrew) for him

I do believe the appropriate person with God's wisdom and power can be the savior (with smalls)

Ezer Kenegdo means helper, helpmate.

Ezer means to rescue, to save, and to be strong.

Kenegdo means suitable for him or corresponding for him

Ezer - the combination of 2 root words "rescue" "save" & "be strong" "savior" We are not only his helper or his companion but rather intended to his savior his deliverer

A leader (husband, man of the house) needs help (rib, wife) and doesn't know it and the help (rib, wife) doesn't know she needs a leader (husband, structure)

Remember sisters, only a rib can strengthen a man, not a side piece.

Meditation Moment

Why do you desire to be a wife?

What form of submissiveness will you give to your husband?

In your time of singleness, how are you preparing to be a wife?

Do you have a prayer life?
Are you equipped in warfare?

How are you spending habits?

Are you ready to submit your body and will to the husband for the Glory of God?

Prepare to be a wife before you get a husband!

I Am HIs Suitable Helper

Chapter 8

~Be a Sister of Light~

If we are to pattern Jesus, then we are to be the light of the world. His light wasn't dim, it wasn't hidden, it wasn't as a light switch either. Jesus' light was BRIGHT & ILLUMINATING!

Matthew 5:14 says YOU are the light of the world, a city that is set on a hill cannot be hid; so, this let us know that we are to have the same BRIGHT light as Jesus did.

I John 2:10 He that loveth his brother or sister abideth in the light, and there is no occasion of stumbling in him - New Living Translation

When your sister comes to you, your responsibility is to be the light.

Psalm 119:105 says
King James Bible
Thy word *is* a lamp unto my feet, and a light unto my path.... let's discuss the difference between a lamp and a light.

A lamp gives light in the space it's needed, a light shed abroad. A light covers more than just a specified space, it covers the whole area. when your sister comes to you with an issue, you are to shed light (Jesus) on that situation and not that of your opinion.

There was an old school Gospel song my Daddy used to sing, "Shine on me, Shine on me, let the light from the lighthouse shine on me." The lighthouse stands in one place but the light searches for miles and miles over the land and the sea.

Some of us are called to be lamps and others are called to be light. The issue with a lot of us today, we don't know our position in the Earth. When things don't look as we think they should be, we offer our" Girl, if I were you..." or "why do you take that?" that is NOT your position. Your position is to be LIGHT, nothing more and nothing less!

Ladies, you have to know that you are prepared for searching deeper into your sister issues (IF she allows and IF the Holy Spirit instructs). We as women take on a lot of things through life; we say that we have dealt with them when we really haven't. We only swept them under the rug. It then begins a pile of unresolved issues, then a molehill, then a mound, and finally a mountain.

His light drives out darkness *John 1:5*

Mediation Moment

In what area of your life is there light?

Are you a lamp or a light? Why?

When was the last time you shed light on your sister's situation?

Do you see yourself and another sister in the female characters that I listed? How can you relate?

Who is the midwife in your life that will help you deliver your promise? Is she trustworthy?

Is there one in your life who will make an exception to the rule?

She provides a roadmap for spiritual direction that helps people understand and exercise their options for Growing in Grace

Chapter 9

~Woman 2 Woman~

1. Ruth & Naomi - We find Ruth, Naomi, and Orpah at the end of their ropes. They are all widows, which at this time in history meant no source of income, and no protection. There was no social security, food banks, welfare, etc. So, when Naomi decided to return back to the House of Bread (Bethlehem), Ruth decided she was going too. Naomi is a sister of Light because she was wise enough to go where provisions were being made for her. She knew that being in Moab, they were under privilege.

Ruth was wise enough to discern the presence and favor of God upon Naomi. So, she says in *Ruth 1:16 & 17*... she said what you got I want it; so, where you lodge, I will lodge, and your people shall be my people. Where you die, I will die and there will I be buried; the Lord do so to me, and more also, if ought but death part you and me.

Orpah on the other hand, decided to go on her own path for provisions. Ladies do not be offended when people do not receive your way of doing things. Many will deliberately rebel against you just because you are _____ (put your name here).

It is nothing that you have done, they are just insecure and jealous. Pray for them that God shows them who they are and keep it moving.

Does the presence dwell in you and is evident as with Naomi? Will you choose to be wise as Ruth to see your sister in the light and follow her until you God says differently?

Will you be wise enough to gleam from someone else's field until you are strong enough to stand on your own?

We understand that the breast is the best source of nutrients and vitamins for a newborn. We are as babes when we first encounter the hurt, the disappointments, the mistakes. The breasts have been said to be a place of power and rest. It is where the child sleeps even during meals. Even men lay on their mothers or wives' breasts for comfort. Children feel protected and comforted on their mother's breast.

If you have ever endured these things, you do as a baby does: cry, whine, complain, and constantly pick at the injury that has been created.

The mother (experienced or seasoned sister) then puts that baby in a comfortable position, normally on the breast to soothe them. As they begin to suck from the mother's breast, they forget about the things that had them crying and upset. In turn, they nestle closer to the Mother because that is their place of comfort and security. Not to sound outlandish in any kind of way, we are to find an experienced woman/mother and suck the nutrients and vitamins from her breast in order to GROW and become stronger from the very thing that tried to take us out.

Breast carry milk, milk is rich and life sustaining for a baby. Leaching onto the right person can save your life!

2. Esther - Esther fought on behalf of her physical family. She found out that Haman was gonna destroy the Jews (her ethnicity) and her Uncle Mordecai. She went unto the King without an invitation, which normally resulted in death. In the end, she saved her people by fasting and letting God be the light to shine in her to the King.

Psalms 68:6

God setteth the solitary in families: he bringeth out those which are bound with chains: but the rebellious dwell in a dry land.

The word solitary means singular or one. In Hebrew, the word is rachid, meaning that one will untie. God often has one person in the family who is serving Him faithfully. Consequently, the salvation of the family is dependent upon that one person. If the light is given to the solitary one, and it is rebuked, the Lord says the rebellious shall dwell in a dry land.

What is your purpose for the family? Are you Moses? Joseph? Joshua? Debra? Mary Magdalene? Rahab?

The sooner you know, the quicker you can get in position for solitaire. A rare cut gem that stands out and has come to mark some of the most significant occasions in one's life. You are that ONE.

3. Jael aka Miss 100 - Jael single-handedly took out an army general with a tent stake. During a battle between the Israelites and the Canaanites, in Judges 4. Jael was a true ride or die chick. Let me make it known, I do not mean it is ok to kill anyone, but I simply mean have someone to go the distance with you.

Jael's story is a metaphor for how we should fight our spiritual battles.

A sister that's down for you, fighting with and for you can be a life saver. Jael didn't allow the disrespect and dishonor. The war wasn't won by this one deed, but with a strong sister beside you, it can happen.

How different would the world look if we seized opportunities, used our resources, freed the oppressed, honored God, and fought like Jael?

4. Priscilla - Priscilla was strong-minded, fervent in her love for God and Jesus Christ, her faith was strong, and she was loyal to her husband - and something of a mover and shaker.

She was trusted by Paul to manage the infant church he left behind, and she taught the gospel as Paul had done. She has listened and observed some of his teaching and he knew that he could trust her to carry on even in his absence.

Let God lead you to a sister that is ever learning from her mistakes, from the Holy Spirit and from life encounters. She will have the intense waters to impart into your life to make you better.

5. Lois & Eunice - *2 Timothy 1*

Godly mothers as sisters

Mothers are great gifts, influencers, proteges, and warriors for our children and families. This Mother/daughter or Mother/daughter in law team raised and esteemed Timothy in GOD. Most women today are only concerned with keeping and loving the Daddy vs. raising and guiding the child as the scriptures have told us to do.

Proverbs 22:6 says Train up a child in THE WAY he/she should go and when he/she is old, he/she will not depart from it.

I purposely capitalized THE WAY because this scripture text has been looked at wrong. Most parents are raising their children the way they were raised, not understanding the misconception of TRAIN UP.

Train up in Hebrew means to consecrate, dedicate

The Word tells us there are two pathways set before us: Death/Life (*Deuteronomy 30:15-20*) or Straight/Narrow (*Matthew 7:13 & 14*).

Just as I believe Lois and Eunice teamed up to bring Timothy into the right PATH of God, so should we!

The generation that is arising now, will not possess the promise just like the Children of Israel. We are failing as parents or better yet adults when it comes to direction. The house must be set in order for the growth to take place.

Teaming up and assisting your sister can lead the youth into a path of righteousness with benefits. Households would never be the same with the insight and wisdom from women with power.

What is your child's purpose? Are you raising them in that pathway?

6. Elizabeth - cousin of Mary (Jesus' Mom)

Make it your priority to find someone with the same goals as you. We know this story found in *Luke 1:39-45*. Mary and Elizabeth were cousins, the genealogy didn't say how or the distance of lineage).

Verse 41 says when Elizabeth HEARD the salutation (greeting; the act of paying respect; as in inquiring of persons welfare, expressing to them kind wishes). The way that Mary greeted Elizabeth caused the baby that she was carrying to leap, and she was FILLED WITH THE HOLY SPIRIT. As they were both pregnant, the one that showed up caused the promise to leap in someone else. This is the kind of sister that I desire to be around.

The word FILLED in the Greek text is "pletho" and it means to imbue, influence or supply, made full

Lots of women gather to gossip, be vindictive and cause chaos, but with the right woman/sister in your corner, your promise and purpose will begin to leap. Her conversation will cause your mind to SHIFT. Your thirst for her words, her strategy, her teachings will have you on a different level mentally and socially.

Verse 44 For lo, as soon as the voice of your salutation sounded in my ears, the babe leaped in the womb for joy, We all are carrying precious cargo, who do you trust and need to not only cause your baby to leap, but to bring to fruition what God has invested in you? There is a sound that is needed for the birth of your baby.

The sound will cause you to contract and begin to nest for the arrival of what's to come. Preparing for the arrival of a baby (promise) requires an environment that is conducive to creative decision making. Parents do not bring their babies home to a dirty house with strangers who are smoking. No, you make sure all things are in order. We do not need people around us who are unstable, gossipers, dream killers, unsupportive, etc.

Who do you need to make you better? wiser? richer? be it financially or in knowledge. I now connect with people who are in the arena of business that I operate in. I listen to them, take notes, read books, and apply these applications to my life and businesses.

If we desire those honest and influential people in our lives, let's learn from them on all levels.

Make sure that your wineskin is worth the pouring of their oil.

Midwives in the Spirit
Exodus 1:15-22

15-16 The king of Egypt had a talk with the two Hebrew midwives; one was named Shiphrah and the other Puah. He said, "When you deliver the Hebrew women, look at the sex of the baby. If it's a boy, kill him; if it's a girl, let her live."

17-18 But the midwives had far too much respect for God and didn't do what the king of Egypt ordered; they let the boy babies live. The king of Egypt called in the midwives. "Why didn't you obey my orders? You've let those babies live!"

19 The midwives answered Pharaoh, "The Hebrew women aren't like the Egyptian women; they're vigorous. Before the midwife can get there, they've already had the baby."

20-21 God was pleased with the midwives. The people continued to increase in number–an extraordinarily strong person. And because the midwives honored God, God gave them families of their own.

22 So Pharaoh issued a general order to all his people: "Every boy that is born, drown him in the Nile. But let the girls live."

When your sister is pregnant naturally or spiritually, you must be there to help her endure the process. Remember, pregnancy has 3 trimesters. Your role as a midwife is particularly important to your sister (the one God has assigned to you). Each thing that she endures may require you and someone else to ensure the baby (Promise) is birthed.

Being on assignment with the right person in the right season grants favor. There will be things that can only come to you with the right connection.

Learning to discern spirits will ultimately be your best friend. We do know our intuition speaks volume but know when the Holy Spirit is speaking trumps intuition any day.

This connection isn't so much about friendship but doing the Divine Will of the Master. I dare not say it can turn into a friendship of sistership, but some assignments are meant to complete the agenda and move on. Allowing feelings to get in the way of that can abort the mission that God has set us on.

Be mindful of the words that you use when ministering to and/or helping a sister. Soul ties and strongholds are real!

Vows, commitments and agreements: Vows are known to bind the soul (*Numbers 30:2*), marriage itself consists of vows and binds the two people together (*Ephesians 5:31*), therefore, I have little reason to overlook the concept of vows or commitments as being a means to create a soul tie.

Chapter 10

~Putting Yourself in Her Shoes~

Perfecting as a Sister *You, therefore, must be perfect [growing into complete maturity of godliness in mind and character, having reached the proper height of virtue and integrity], as your heavenly Father is perfect.*
–Matthew 5:48

A blood/biological sister sometimes can be different from one who you have acquired over the years. However, for many the one who isn't biological becomes that of blood relation. I do understand that the reputation of women has lessened over the years. I also understand that women can heal properly with another woman's help; especially once she has been delivered and set free.

Perfect - /pər'fekt/

make (something) completely free from faults or defects, or as close to such a condition as possible.

Women have a nurturing spirit that can shift any person or any atmosphere. Our tone, our touch and our speech can soothe a person. Examining the good, bad, and indifference in our daily walk ministers to us and others.

The word rendered "perfecting" (akin to the "perfection") is derived from a root which signifies either to "mend" what is broken (as in *Matthew 4:21*), or to "complete" what is unfinished, and hence is used spiritually for to "restore" the fallen (*Galatians 6:1*).

Perfect in the unity of the faith, &, ought rather to be rendered, to the unity, or union, of the faith, or that union which is the fruit or consequence of the faith, namely, of perfect faith, even the faith spoken of by our Lord in his intercessory prayer, recorded *John 17:20-23*, where he says, I pray for them which shall believe on me, that they all may be one, as thou Father art in me and I in thee, that they may be made perfect in one, that is, may be perfectly united in love to us and one another.

I declare I am free from low self-esteem, hurt, anger, bitterness, jealousy, and resentment. God has given me the power to root out, pull down, destroy, and to throw down these things so they may never place seed in my life again

I take dominion over these and now successfully plant love, peace, high self-esteem, integrity, morals, and build a long-lasting legacy for my children to inherit.

Jeremiah 1:10

I am being perfected for the work of the ministry of Jesus Christ.

Mediation Moment

In what areas have you been perfected?

What areas do you struggle with? Have you asked God to break up the fallow ground of your heart concerning your struggles?

Can you relate to Hosea 10:2? Where is your relationship with God today?

What emotions do you need to work on, so your heart remains pure?

What has unforgiveness done to your heart?

Declare I am an Agent of Change.

Chapter 11

~The Heart of a Sister~

The Bible tells us in *Jeremiah 17:9* - The human heart is the most deceitful of all things, and desperately wicked. Who really knows how bad it is? New Living Translation

Break up the fallow ground of the heart- Land was allowed to lie fallow that it might become more fruitful; but when in this condition, it soon became overgrown with thorns and weeds. The cultivators of the soil were careful to "break up" his fallow ground, i.e., to clear the field of weeds, before sowing seed in it.

So says the prophet, "Break off your evil ways, repent of your sins, cease to do evil, and then the good seed of the word will have room to grow and bear fruit."

There are always areas in our lives that need breaking up. I don't care how Holy and Righteous we know to act, there is always a struggle of flesh and spirit in our daily walk.

Why does God speak in Hosea about this? This is a picture of a land that used to be known for its righteousness but has now turned from God and grown cold toward Him. As with our hearts, this is supposed to be the place of God's sitting.. in the Heart (spirit) but we have allowed things to contaminate since we have not dealt with those things.

We must deal with those things in our heart against our sisters. We tend to let the things that are incomplete in our lives build up into hate, bitter, jealousy, and malice. This causes the heart to become dark and black, pushing God's love out. His love must be a constant for the people of God, no matter how hard it is.

He commanded us to LOVE our neighbor as yourself. Yes, true enough the enemy will send someone to pull you out of position. We truly need to seek God for the protection of our emotions. If the enemy sees he can plant one seed into our emotional field and we water it (meditate on it), it's over.

What do I mean by water? Worrying about it, meditating on it, keeping it in open conversation about what your sister/husband/mother/co-worker did and did not do.

The more it takes root in you, the darker you become and before you know it is a seed of bitterness. *Hebrews 12:8* Looking diligently lest any man fall of the Grace of God; lest any root of bitterness springing up trouble and thereby many be defiled.

To try to live for God after His prescribed order, which is the Cross and everything He did on the Cross, will bring nothing but failure; thereby providing fertile ground for roots of bitterness and begin to speak the words of the flesh.

Forgiving quickly is the key!! I had to learn the hard way that unforgiveness hinders prayers, keeps you bound, sets you behind in destiny, and can physically make you sick.

Experts say that bitterness and unforgiveness can indeed make us sick and even kill us. Some believe unforgiveness causes cancer in the body.

Unforgiveness can hinder our faith. You can't possibly see the things hoped for and evidence of things not seen if you know you or a person needs forgiveness.

Leviticus 19:17 You must not harbor hatred against your brother in your heart (inner man, spirit). Directly rebuke your neighbor, so that you will not incur guilt on account of him. The enemy is crafty, and he knows what upset you, he knows what gets under your skin, he knows what makes you nervous/anxious and he also knows what will in the long run make you bitter.

Jesus says that the heart's secrets are betrayed by the mouth, even as a tree's fruit discloses its nature (*Matthew 12:33-34*)

Be watchful.

Listen.

Examine the fruit.

Notes

Notes

_____

_____

_____

_____

_____

_____

_____

_____

_____

_____

_____

_____

_____

_____

_____

_____

_____

_____

Notes

_____
_____
_____
_____
_____
_____
_____
_____
_____
_____
_____
_____
_____
_____
_____
_____
_____
_____

Notes

Notes

CONNECTION

I pray that the words of this booklet have given you new hope, new peace and a new direction in life. Continue to stay in Him, know who you are and walk worthy of the vocation

Therefore, the prisoner of the Lord, beseech you that ye walk worthy of the vocation wherewith ye are called, with all lowliness and meekness, with longsuffering, forbearing one another in love – Ephesians 4:1-2 (KJV)

Evangelist Sherry Eaton

Fear Nothing Ministries, established September 1998

Licensed into Ministry, November 2012

Facebook
Fear Nothing Ministries
https://www.facebook.com/EvangelistEaton/

Sherry Eaton - Seven Mogul
https://www.facebook.com/MessengerSherryEaton

Website:
www.sevenmogul.com

www.ingramcontent.com/pod-product-compliance
Lightning Source LLC
Chambersburg PA
CBHW071100090426
42737CB00013B/2404